Antoni Gaudí

"Creation continues unceasingly through the media of Man. But Man does not create, he discovers. Those who search for the Laws of Nature as a support to their new works collaborate with the Creator. Copiers do not collaborate. Therefore, orginality consists in returning to the origin."

"The more perfect the shape, less ornamentation is necessary."
"Imitation of styles needs superfluous ornamentation, simple styles are those which have a good structure."

"Elegance is the sister of poverty but poverty should not be confused with misery."

"The ideal quality of a work of art is harmony which, in the plastic arts, is born from light giving relief and decoration. Architecture distributes the light."

A. Gaudí

EDITORIAL
A. CAMPAÑA EDITIONS
C/Alcalde de Móstoles, 19 – 08025 BARCELONA
Tel. (3493) 4564336 Fax: (3493) 4501889
PHOTOGRAPHY
Antoni Campañá Capella
Paco Largo
Pepe Encinas

STAMP
FUTURGRAFIC

PHOTOMECHANIC
JEBA

ISBN: 84-86294-7-0   legal diposit: B-36.523-XLIII

Antoni Gaudí i Cornet was born on 25th June, 1852, in the city of Reus- the second largest city in Catalonia in that period- of a family of coppersmiths. The originality and profound character of his works have made him and his creations a theme of continued controvesy. In reference to Gaudí himself, it has been said that humanity only produces original, new architecture which can change everything every seven or eight centuries. This is true when faced with the works and figure of Gaudí, understanding that hidden behind an outflow of imagination and creativity characteristic to him, there is a complete and coherent,

SCHOOLS.

University auditorium, presented by Gaudi as a project for his final examination

Project for a cemetary door.

harmonious and monolithic conception of society and Man, of politics and religion and, in short of architecture which served his deep convictions. The most universal architect which Catalonia gave to the world was the last of five brothers and although he did not follow the traditional occupation of his family, he always declared and recognised his own personal conception of space and volumn in the profession of his father.In the construction of the boilers which his father made, Gaudí saw a free treatment, almost immaterial, of space, not subject to rules other than the malleability of material and will of the hands, serving a natural need or function.

Faced with the work of Gaudí a fundimental question is raised, frivolity or sincerity, vanity or silence? Overflowing imagination and disregard for traditional rules, characteristic to Gaudí, have permitted us to think that we find ourselves faced with the work of a visionary or madman. More than three quarters of a century later it seems absurd to mantain the superficial vision of his work. Gaudí was treated unjustly, misunderstood by the majority of his contempories.

To understand the results achieved by Gaudí one must place oneself in the agony of the Romantic period, Neoclassic models and also in the geographic space where he lived, loved and fully understood, in that period of renovation: the cities of Reus and Barcelona. It was the explosion of Art Nouveau, the movement which regenerated and redefined the arts which could be produced by the person and his work. Even so, it should also be pointed out that Gaudí-always connected with his historic moment and his people- ahead of his time never limited himself to any school of criteria, which makes him and his work a chapter apart in Art Nouveau (also known as Modern Syle, Sezessionstil, Style 1900). After his first studies in Reus, Gaudí moved to Barcelona where he began and completed the career of architect, paid for by his father who, to be able to do this, had to sell a small property. During all his career he alternated study with professional collaboration with several architects in Barcelona. Once he had his degree, he continued these collaborations and he worked on the ornamentation of "Cuidadela" Park, Barcelona, the Ladychapel for the Virgin of Montserrat, the street lamps in "Plaza Real", Barcelona, Vincens House, the co-operative "La Oberera Mataronense" and the furniture for "Comillas" chapel, as well as other diverse projects not always carried out.These were his first trials in finding solutions - synthesis of Romanic-Gothic Medievalism, organic

Plaza Real. One of the models for street lamps, projected in the first period.

naturalism, orientalism, geometry - which make up all his later works. The diversity of his assignments is evident and would be mantained in everything this architect produced; town planning, decorative,

Ciudadela Park.
Above, the great cascade.
Gaudi collaborated in both
the hydraulic and architectural
project. Below an ornamental
motif for the entrance gates.
Gaudi's
collaboration in the building
project
of the park meant the first
experience in
town planning, an aspect
which would
later lead to the construction
of housing
for factory workers for the "La
Obrera
Mataronense"cooperative. The
other large
project of town planning would
be the garden-
city, Park Güell. Iron, present
in all of Gaudi's
work, is already visible in the
columns crowned
by helmets, as in the street
lamps of the Plaza
Real. In this case the elements
are cast; in later
works wrought iron takes
precedence.

private, social or religious.
The words of Antoni Gaudí at the
beginning of this book, contain all his
thoughts and thus allow us to synthesise
the great effort which coincides in all his
work, organic naturalism, tied to earth
and Mankind; a sense of geometry and
the movement of space; functional use

of space without harming greatness; considering the work as a coherente whole to the service of the deepest conviction about Man. After all this the constant parables appear, the use of material belonging to that period, (iron, concrete) combined with a new treatment of the already traditional ones (bricks, stone, mosaic), the sober Arabesque geometry and elements of a very much alive fabulous nature. Between 1887 and 1906, that is a period of nineteen years, Gaudí planned and built the palace of Astorga,

On the left Güell Pavillions, built
between 1885 and 1888, shortly
before the first Universal Exhibition
of Barcelona. The aerial view allows
contemplation of the new conception
of space, recesses and projections,
vaults, crowns which characterize
Gaudi's work.

On the right, the wrought iron
of the main entrance reminds
one of the vigilant dragon, the
legend of Saint George, patron
of Catalonia

Below detail of the benches.
The ostentation of the
mosaic corroborates
the oriental character of the
work.

The "Botines de Léon" house and the houses, "Figueres de Bellesguard", "Calvet" and "Batlló" in Barcelona. The assignments were numerous and of a certain importance and if nothing went wrong they were finished within a reasonable time. Think that the great college of the Teresianes was finished in only two years. The palace of Astorga was a project which Gaudí himself could not finish, reforms were necessary for several reasons and that, as has

Palacio Güell in Nou de la Rambla street. This sumptuous residence, paradoxically contempory of the "Teresinas" convent, represents the consolidation of the author's resources. In the interior, as on the facades and exteriors, imagination competes with sumptuousness, solidness with elegance. Above, a detail of the interior. Above right, the roof with integrated ventilators and chimnies. Eusebio Güell, who received the title of Count, was one of the most notable figures of that period. The comfortable position he enjoyed allowed him to be a real patron in cultural life. His relationship with Antoni Gaudí, a true and continuous friendship, put at the service of the architect every freedom, and means for the projection and execution of the numberous works which made them inseperable.
On the right a cross section of the Palacio Güell and two aspects of the same.

Antoni Gaudí. Palau Güell. Barcelona. Secció transversal. 1886.

"The more perfect the shape, less ornamentation is necessary."

"Imitation of styles needs superfluous ornamentation, simple styles are those which have a good structure."
Antoni Gaudí.
Diary. (Fragments published in "Nueva visión de Gaudí" by E.Casanelles.)

Four aspects of the Teresinas college. (Ganduxer street, next to Ronda del Mig). On Art Nouveau ideals inspired in the naturalism of Ruskin, this works dispenses with the ornamental elements in favour of simple expresion of form. On the facing page, a detail of the cloister from the corridor. Above, a view of the whole main body. Below a crown and wrought iron, present in all of Gaudi's work, a motive more allegorical than decorative

Episcopal Palace of Astorga. This work, the fruit of a project in which he had to resolve many difficulties, is an attempt to combine the Medieval tradition of the kingdom of Leon with the legend, allegory and use of all natural resources

Casa de los Botines, León. This work is the materialization and consolidation of Gaudí's civil style. With the use of his habitual materials, this work offers a solid whole, coherent, strong, imaginative and measured.

"El Capricho Comillas" (Comillas folly) Conceived in an Arabesque style, very similar to Casa Vicens. This work was not directed by Gaudí personally. The project, still in his juvenile period, is a true example of his will to break away and represents Art Nouveau, overflowing with solutions or creative artifice, exotic inspiration, within popular reach, connecting as he did the strange with the same.

Above another novel work of Antoni Gaudí, the Güell cellars in Garraf.

been said, allows the most varied interpretation. Elements leaning towards integrating the house into the surrounding countryside appear, Biertzo granite, the characteristics of a fortress and the use of pottery from the same district. Not the most representative work of the author, it possesses an attractiveness - the medieval features, a legendary flavour- which distinguishes this monumental work.

The "Botines de León" house is related to the work of Astorga and to the great friendship between Gaudí and Güell. It is

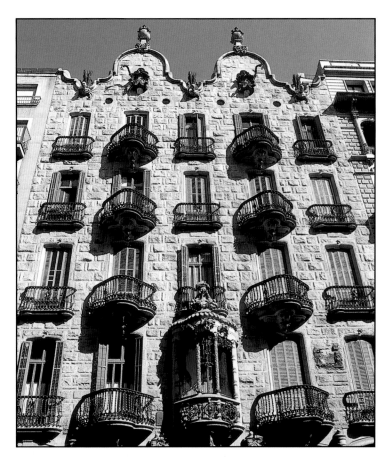

"Casa Calvet" is in the middle of the Barcelona "ensanche" on a very limited site and shows some solutions not yet definite, but full of meaning for a town house destined to be family apartments. The photo shows the posterior facade.

On the right an apect of the door to "Finca Miralles".

Door to "Finca Miralles", in Paseo de Manel Girona, built in 1901. In principal the project was to be for a complete housing development.

a solid and sober pile where the use of worked stone gives the facades the articulated character of authentic relief. There is a great distance between this work and the earlier works of the author, who here combines a large compact structure with light imaginative elements. Ornamentation using wrought iron reappears and for the first time in a private building, the architect uses it as a sculptured element - Saint George - integrated into the whole. The figure presides over the main door. The whole inscribes the most personal line of the architect, who in this project, had complete freedom to resolve, through decoration, the best way to protect the interior from the hard climate of León. The Gothic line already used in the

project of the "Sagrada Familia" is maintained in the works of Astorga, León and the one which he built for the Figueres family between 1900 and 1902 - the classical two years which Gaudí dedicated to each new project. It was known by the name of "Bellesguard", the disappeared Royal residence of the Catalan-Aragonese Crown in the "Bonanova" in Barcelona. This Gothic line had, however, been interrupted in Calvet house, in Caspe street in the Barcelona "ensanche". A work with echoes of Baroque, the facade in worked stone as in "Botines" house and the use of wrought iron which Gaudí values as a fundamental support.. Both the anterior facade as the interior one of "Calvet" house, built on a limited site, are

Majorca Cathedral, restored between 1904 and 1913. Returns the unadorned luminosity to the temple, the space and character deprived the central presbytery by large, walled off windows and alterpieces which hid the work. Gaudi, with Jujol conceived the lyrical-aerial baldoquin and several elements for the new presbytery.

Casa Vincens (Las Carolina street, Gracia), geometric style inspired in arabesque architecture, which successfully tries to incorporate colour and is an obvious break with the canons of the period. It was built for a manufacturer of mosaic.

are interesting . The volumns present a very advanced treatment for the period. The interior decoration is of equal importance as can be seen by only going into the entrance to the house. "Bellesguard" house, with no limitation of space, returns to Gothic inspiration, perhaps in memory of the period of maximum splendor of the Catalan dynasty which had a recreational palace here. Fantasy reappears in this compact and, at the same time, delicate residence.

Casa Figueras de Bellesguard from a corner of the garden. The house was built between 1900 and 1909.

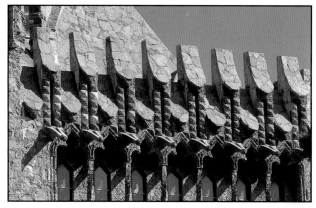

Crown on the facade
making a rail with the
terrace. Covered
windows form a
gallery to illuminate the loft.

Detail of a wrought iron door and the lateral, ceramic
benches in Casa Figueres de Bellesguard.
A private house conceived to recall the summer palace
of the Catalan-Aragon Crown which,
now disappeared, stood in this same place, with a view
over the Barcelona of the XVC, now lost.

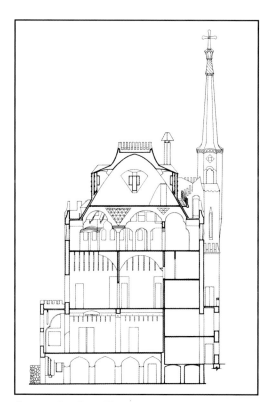

Cross section of casa Figueres

Detail of the bench in Casa Figueres.

First image of the whole of the Sagrada Familia temple, seen from the facade of the Nativity, according to the drawing by Juan Rubío i Bellver made in 1906.

When Gaudí took charge of the project for the Expiatory Temple of the "Sagrada Familia" (Holy Family) he was only thirty-one. It was one of his first assignments and, without a doubt, the most important one. The site had been purchased by the Association of Devotees of Saint Joseph in 1881 and the architect Del Villar, with whom Gaudí had collaborated on several occasions, had been asked to carry out the project. The work was begun in 1882. Del Villar declined to continue and passed it to Joan Martorell, a fundamentally religious architect, who gave the assignment to his ex-helper, Gaudí. Gaudí never abandoned this huge work which he could never finish, as he himself recognised, because of this he alternated work on the project

The facade of the Nativity presents several degrees in architecural and sculptural relief
which constitutes the whole wall.

The three illustrations offer different aspects of the only facade which Gaudí knew, the Nativity. The great tableau of stone is a combination of architecture, sculpture and colour. To carry out the project, Gaudí counted on the collaboration of stone masons, potters, blacksmiths, architects who understood the work and penetrated in the spirit which the architect stamped on it constantly. The last statues on the door are the work of the Japanese sculptor Etzuro Sotoo.

with other assignments. It fell behind the first works already mentioned, Vicen's house -which Gaudí built for a manufacturer of mosaics-the "Capricho de Comillas"(Comillas folly), alterations were made in 1925 with his authority, and more than one unfulfilled project. On taking charge of the "Sagrada Familia", Gaudí was conditioned by several circumstances, the site and arrangement of the New Cathedral of Barcelona, the small part of the works already begun and,

A raised drawing of the whole project of the Sagrada Familia from the facade of the Passion. Finally the door and its ornamentation has been made by he sculptor Josep Maria Subirachs who has stamped his own style on it.

more importantly, the founders and their construction board to whom he found himself subjected. The "Sagrada Familia" is the masterpiece of the architect but not the most personal creation of Gaudí. On one occasion, in reference to the way of carrying out the work, he explained that not all was owed to his will nor less to his whim, but to circumstances not imposed by him but to which he had to yield.On the death of Gaudí in 1926, the architects Domènec Sugranyes and Francesc P. Quintana, took over the work and finished the four belltowers, In 1939 the architects Isidre Puig Boada and Lluis Bonet i Galí joined the project and began the reconstruction of

In the upper photograph the four towers and part of the facade of the Passion and as well as the advanced works of the central nave of the Sagrada Familia with the entrance orientated to Mallorca street.

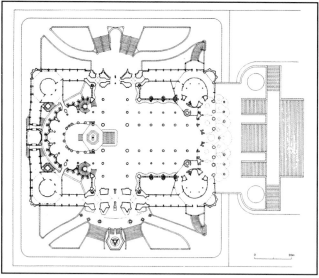

Plan of the whole temple of the Sagrada Familia, where we can appreciate the three doors and the distribution of the central nave, in construction.The most modern computer techniques are being used to follow Gaudí's design as closely as possible.

the models. In 1971 Lluís Bonet i Galí took charge of the works. In 1985 the architect Jordi Bonet i Armengol took over and one year later the sculptor Josep María Subirachs began the facade of the Passion.

Currently the Temple presents two of the three facades on which he had to count. The facade of the Nativity was already finished with the four towers which crown it, in Gaudí's lifetime. That of the Passion has recently been finished. Orientated to the south-side, facing the sea- the facade of the Glory must be built higher than the other two. This group of twelve towers - four on each facade - will symbolize the twelve Apostles. Another four towers, higher than the previous

In the Sagrada Familia, the use of some Gothic style models are only a pretext on which Gaudí could develop his imagination in the service of his thought and faith. The contrast of the interior and exterior facades of the Nativity make this treatment of style obvious. On this page three aspects of the interior of this facade which will connect to the central nave to build the interior of the temple.

ones, will represent the four Evangelists surrounding a great central spire, symbol of the Saviour. Above the aspe there will be a elevated cupola in representation of the Virgin.

The "Sagrada Familia", the most permanent and ambitious project of the author, will have all the variety of solutions and recourses

which Gaudí adopted during his profession and his life. In this way the constrast between the interior and exterior facades is very marked. The general shape of these immense articulated walls comes from a Neo-Gothic conception- in part conditioned by the wishes of the board of the temple- the front and reverse facade of the Nativity offers two completely different visions; the exterior face, a great profusion, almost Baroque, of statuary, vegetable and organic elements; the interior, a pleasing interpretative treatment of geometry and the play of volumns, something which speaks

Four aspects of the new phase of construction of the Sagrada Familia Temple. On the right a view of the nave, exterior and interior. On the right the interior and a detail of the columns.

of a constructivist Neo-Gothic, an unsurprising experience with Gaudí but totally unusual and new. In the "Sagrada Familia", as in the greater

On the left the interior of a tower where we can see the total organic development. The banister and spiral staircase offer another example of the simplicity which Gaudí uses to resolve a problem such as mobility inside the bell towers. Below plans of the connected towers and section.

part of his works, Gaudí counted on an active and direct collaboration with architects, sculptors, potters, stone-masons, etc. They were always people who understood Gaudí intimately and absolutely, and the architect frequently trusted their initiative and solutions. Among these architects we mention Berenguer and Jujol, constant collaborators in the work of Gaudí.

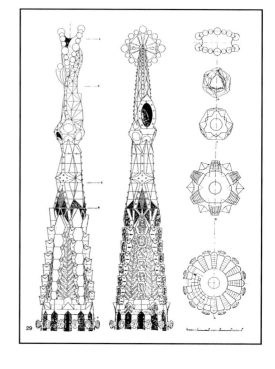

29

Three aspects of the towers and their crowns, where we can see the organic harmony and the combination of elements which project the ascendant and transcendent nature of the bell towers, in search of height.

Above a model of the Sagrada Familia.
Gaudí did not make a detailed,
completed project of the work, so
the current work always
follows, wherever possible, the
numerous notes,
suggestions, the model and in the
background tries to be faithful
to the spirit of Gaudí
and "Barcelona Cathedral".
Below, a detail of ornamentation.

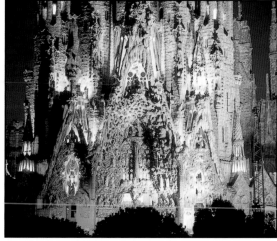

Above, an aerial view of the Sagrada Familia. The work was begun in 1884 and continues after more than a century, having passed through economic difficulties. Currently two of the three facades, the Nativity and the Passion are finished and the Glory is under construction. On the right the facade of the Nativity at night.

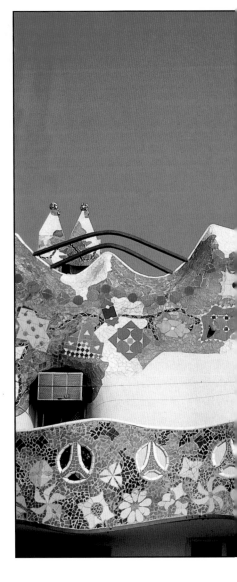

Three aspects of the posterior facade of "Casa Batlló" For Gaudí a esthetic and functionality were his main concern therefore, the posterior part of town houses should not be lacking in harmony and sense of the building being a whole. The extraordinary colouring of the finishing converts the roofs into authentic creations where he devellops his implacable fantasy. The remodelling done by Gaudí to "casa Batlló" was carried out between 1906 and 1909.

Antoni Gaudí was a profoundly religious man. Determined circumstances gave him the opportunity to specialise in the field of architecture in the service of the church. We recall the work he did in Montserrat, the Teresiana college, the episcopal palace of Astorga and the crypt of Santa Coloma de Cervelló, his most personal work. Another great chapter of Gaudí's works is that of the works for Count Güell. With these two indications we can see that, leaving to one side the personal religiousness of the man, his work was, as in so many other cases, fruit of the nature

Casa Batlló (Paeo de Gracia-Aragon street). The improvements to a previous building helped Gaudí compose a facade suggestive of back of the legendary dragon of the patron of Catalonia, Saint George.

organic strength on an almost animal tissue which recalls the

On the right, two
aspects of the main
facade, with original
balconies and splendid
colour of this original
work of Gaudí.

On the left, interior of casa Battló where the integral concept of Gaudí's work is reflected.

of his assignments but always a result of his personal singularity. What would have been the result if his work had followed the town plannning experience of the working class district in Mataró? Probably similar, but with a distinct finality and orientation. The expressive strength with which Gaudí conceived space in the service of Mankind would always have shone through. The "Batlló" house in "Paseo de Gracia", organic and at the same time lyrical, respondes to the assignment of transformation and dignity of a

Above the large window of the main facade of casa Batlló, which clearly demonstrates how he copied natural elements. In this case in the shape of human bones.

Below, two details of the interior of casa Batlló.

A detail of the wrought iron on the main door to the area, a semiserialized motif where Gaudí once again returns to one of the oldest techniques

Below the smiling dragon of Saint George, with the Catalan flag in the background, it presides over the steps.

Park Güell (above Travasera de Dalt and Sanlleh square, metro development of middle class family houses of the period. The pr a municipal park. In the photo the main entrance.

conventional house. Over the anterior structure, Gaudí articulated and reformed the facades, the public interior spaces and the main floor for which he planned furniture according to its style, today in the Gaudí museum.

Count Güell, a notable and almost perpetual client and friend of Gaudí planned the construction of a residential park on the outskirts of the city. the structure of the estate came into being between 1900 and 1914 under the direction of the architect. The conception of a residential area with the characteristics foreseen by Güell was far in advance of the Catalonia of that time.

Pavillion at the entrance to Park Güell with Gaudí's double cross.

Above, the original steps outside the building at the entrance to Park Güell, decorated in ceramic. On the right the large windows

The main entrance, steps, presided over by a fountain, a truely beautiful, smiling dragon in polychrome ceramic. Behind the dragon we can see the columns of the "hipostila" hall which supports the great square and a bench also covered in ceramic below the columns.

The project failed, only two of the proposed seventy houses were built. The new neighbourhood would have had a market, church, public services pavillion as well as the services, relatively modern then, of electricity, running water etc. The restrictions imposed on construction of the houses limited building to favour landscaping, reduced height to assure full enjoyment of the

The "hipostila" or hall of columns meant to be a market place according to the housing project designed by Gaudí.

The hall of columns which supports the great square and the vaulted ceiling representing an abdomen decorated with magnificent medallions of polychromed ceramic, by Jujol, an intimate collaborator of Gaudí.

Above a circular colonnade supports the great square, surrounded by a monumental bench. The fragmented tiles, unique material of the bench is a first in modern art. Every corner offers a bright, painting with all the luminosity of enamalled mosaic.

Several aspects of the long walk under the viaduct. The vaults are decorated with stalactites. The capitels of the sloping columns which support the viaduct are like giant clinging limpits.

sun, etc. - made the project a dream deserving of Gaudí's enthusiasm. The architect put all his creative capacity into the work at the service of a company with undoubtable social scope and open future.

The elements which were built - the pavillions of the entrance with columns which was destined to become the market, the viaducts, the prodigious monumental bench, constitute a true synthesis of the arts:

Above a detailed view of the entrance steps where the white mosaic stands out and crowned by the terrace which leads to the park's gardens.

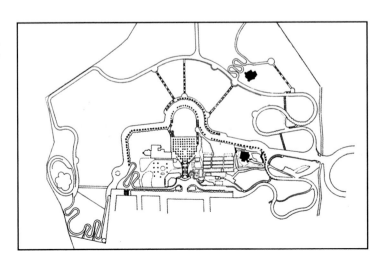

This is the plan, which Gaudí made for Park
Güell on the "so-called"
Bald Mountain, in 1900.

Several aspects of the raised accesses which run through the park. Vegetable and mineral ornamentation, integral in the nature of a garden city, the great proposal of Antoni Gaudí.

architecture, sculpture, painting, forging, pottery and gardening. Everything combined in this possible dream which even included a great Theatre of Nature, a new type of Greek Theatre. The project began sinuously from the mountainous terrain, to which it was adapted with gardens and different levels. The works we can see today have been there for fourteen years.

In the first stage (1900-1903) almost all the buildings were finished, with the important exception of the serpentine bench, one of Gaudí's most important works. The bench, a powerful prelude to the paintings of Miró and the Art tendency of today, combines the work of all Gaudí's collaborators, always under the architect's supervision.

On the left one of the pavillions at the entrance to Park Güell designed for the administration service. Here the basic elements which Gaudí selected for the construction of the park are combined with original works such as a vent inside a ceramic cross.

What has popularly been called "cathedral of fragments" ("catedral de trancadis") was the first experience with what has later been called "collage". Gaudí and his collaborators assessed in depth every finish, every detail, in recovering old mosaics with all the tones of fantasy. Critics have coincided in praising the bench in Güell Park and the one in the crypt of Güell de Cervelló as the highest monuments to Antoni Gaudí.

Above and below the pinnacles which top the buildings at the entrance to Park Güell. Below right, a view of the Gaudí Museum, a house where he spent the last days of his life, which reflects the proposal for a housing project within a garden which he designed as a model of town planning.

Main facade of casa Milá.

A perspective of casa Milá from Provenca street where the undulation of the balconies can be observed.

Before his death Gaudí lived his last years in a small house in Park Güell. He died in Barcelona 10th July, 1926 after having been run over by a tram. Behind each work of Gaudí there is a unitary conception and almost always codes which transcend architecture itself. Up to that moment the civil work of the

Casa Milá, named or known as "La Pedrera" (Paseo de Gracia-Provenza). A block for family housing in the centre of the city, built between 1906 and 1910. Below, a detail of the wrought iron finishing of the balconies.

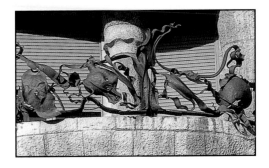

architect, more or less fantastic, evocative, creative had been limited to rules of use. The "Pedrera"- a popular name for "Casa Milá" - frankly breaks those rules. How much of a religious work has this house, begun in 1906? The intitial project forsaw building a complete block of houses and not only the fragment which was

Above, an aerial view of the Pedrera. The corner facade and the terrace where we can observe the original wells and the no less surprising chimnies and ventilators. On the left, the chimnies, ventilators and vents which crown Casa Milá.

Above the vents which
populate and animate the
surface of Casa Milá.
On the right, surrealistic
and vigilant ventilators.

finished. The whole was to have been a giant pedestal for a figure of the Virgin with which Gaudí planned to preside over the whole block. The richness and variety of recourses developed in this work make commentary impossible. The work, in spite of the great revolutionary innovations which he introduced was strongly attacked by intellectuals of the period who

Two aspects of the Crypt of Colonia Güell in Santa Coloma de Cervelló, part of a large housing project which was thwarted in 1914.

considered too daring what is now considered the maximum expression of Catalan Art Nouveau.

Due to the I World War in 1914 and the death in 1918, of the Count, promotor of the project, only the crypt of the project for the Güell colony church of "Santa Coloma de Cervello" was completed. The church, together with the crypt was destined exclusively to

The church in Colonia Güell inspired by a mountainous formation. Comparison with the "Agulles de Travesany" in the Pyrenees.

Stalactites in the caves of Drach in Majorca and the towers of the Sagrada Familia.

Tower of the service pavillion in Park Güell and the trunk of a palm tree.

A Chimney of Casa Milá and a conch.

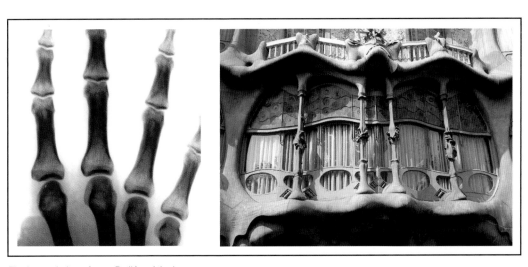

The large window of casa Batlló and the human skeleton.

The shape of a cypress tree is similar to the towers of the Sagrada Familia.

The mountain of Montserrat was also a motive of inspiration for Antoni Gaudí.

PROJECTS NOT CARRIED OUT.

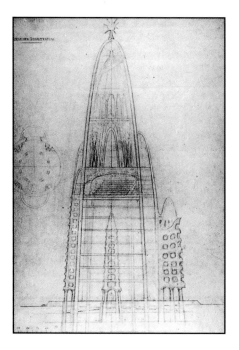

Cross section of
a project for a hotel
in New York, 1908.

Elevation of a project for Catholic Missions
in Tangier, 1892.

religious services for the adjacent working class development. It is the second case where Güell and Gaudí devoted themselves to a plan of immense social dimensions; here a working class neighbourhood, in Güell Park a housing project for the middle classes. The crypt depicts the experience and culminates the anterior work of the architect.

The integration of this work into the countryside has repeatedly been commented, the employment of the materials best loved by Gaudí, the treatment of light in the interior spaces - covered or in the open air - and the lively rythm in this building-vaults, columns - constitute the material expression of the desire of Man to project himself in transcendency.